Hacking Made Simple

I0012850

The Beginners Guide To Hacking: Learn The Basics of Hacking in 24 Hours

By Kiril Valtchev

Copyright 2016

TABLE OF CONTENTS

CHAPTER 4: STEP BY STEP PROCEDURES

INTRO

Why are you here? What drove your curiosity? Why do you want to learn about this? These are all questions that you **don't** need to know the answer to. Our curiosity can be driven by anything, especially the unknown.

Hacking is an art. Sometimes an honest art and sometimes malicious. This book aims to equip you with the basics of the hacking world. The beginning of this book will to go through what hacking actually is and some of its implications.

The next few chapters dive into some of the commonly known hacking languages, tools, techniques and mentalities that are required in order to be a hacker. Not every person is meant to be a hacker, but everyone can at least learn about it. Being a hacker is no easy task. It requires constant practice, improvement and a willingness to go beyond what is commonly taught.

As the book progresses you will learn that hacking is not something you learn overnight. It takes years to perfect your craft in order to become obsolete. In order to become a great hacker you must develop an insane thirst for information. Information is the primary driver for hackers and it drives the flow of knowledge. Information is the most valuable asset in the world.

Hacking can present huge opportunities in terms of a career choice or it can land you behind bars if you aren't careful. This book serves as an educational tool **ONLY** and is not meant to teach malicious acts of any kind. Learn and use the information presented in this book at your full discretion and remember to be cautious.

Let's Begin!!!

CHAPTER 1: HACKING

What is Hacking?

Before we dive into the world of hacking it is important to define exactly what hacking is. People generally have a skewed misconception of what hacking is. A lot of people automatically default to thinking that hacking is always a malicious act. This is not always the case.

So what is hacking? Hacking is the process of changing the structure or feature of a system in order to change what the system was originally intended to do. A person who constantly tries to penetrate and exploit weaknesses in computer systems or networks in order to gain access is known as a **"hacker"**.

Hackers tend to be sophisticated IT and software engineers with years of experience. They love to solve complex problems and find alternative solutions to anything that can make a process quicker, more efficient, and economically feasible.

TYPES OF HACKERS

Hackers have different classifications depending on what kind of actions they take. Below are some of the commonly known types of hackers.

White Hat Hacker

A white hat hacker is a hacker who gains access to a computer system in order to fix a specific issue or weakness within an organization. They are typically known as **"ethical hackers"**. These are the good guys. They will help remove certain viruses or malicious programs for organizations or individuals.

Black Hat Hacker

A black hat hacker is a hacker who attempts to breach or bypass a computer or secure network in order to cause harm to the network, steal classified information, money, identities and much more. These are the bad and malicious guys you hear about on television. They break into computers and networks to create viruses, spread malware and cause destruction. They are also commonly referred to as **"crackers"**.

Gray Hat Hacker

This is a hacker who ends up violating typical standards and laws, but doesn't have the malicious intent of a black hat hacker. They are sort of in the middle between a white hat hacker and a black hat hacker. Gray hat hackers infiltrate systems with the goal of exposing hidden information or bad people, not to necessarily corrupt files and deploy viruses. They use their skills not for personal gain, but more to prove a specific point or concept. A modern day example of a gray hat is the hacking group Anonymous.

Script Kiddie Cracker

A script kiddie is a person who uses premade programs, scripts or viruses to hack. They really don't have an interest in learning the intricacies of hacking. They just use programs that are already at their disposal or through open source websites in order to hack. Most script kiddies tend to get caught because of their inability to cover their tracks. They are the newbies of the hacking world. They are impulsive and non-serious hackers.

Green Hat Hackers

A green hat hacker is someone who is new to the scene of hacking and is just beginning to learn the basics. They are also considered newbies. They are not like script kiddies because they want to actually learn how hacking works and develop the necessary skills to become proficient.

Blue Hat Hackers

These types of hackers hack for their own personal entertainment or to sabotage and get revenge on someone. They are typically passive for the most part until someone or something angers them. Blue hat hackers are the jealous ex-boyfriends that never got over that breakup. For the most part they don't tend to cause too much mayhem unless seriously provoked.

Red Hat Hackers

Red hat hackers are hackers that are employed by government agencies with the intent to hack or penetrate networks of other government entities. They are used to sniff out potential threats from other governments or entities.

Government entities employ these people to ensure that their infrastructure is kept up to date and maintained to the highest degree in order to prevent any possible attacks from other government organizations. It is not uncommon for black hat hackers to transition to red hats once they are caught.

DIFFERENT FORMS OF HACKING

Hacking will continue to happen on a daily basis throughout the world. There will be ethical hackers and malicious hackers. Ethical hackers will try to protect computer networks and systems from being exploited by malicious hackers. Malicious hackers will try everything they can do gain access to the information they desire. Let's take a look at what the good guys do and what the bad guys try to do.

GOOD HACKING

The internet is an absolute massive network. It is a realm of servers, virtual machines, datacenters and people who make it what it is. Ethical hackers try to protect the infrastructure of networks in order to prevent the networks from being penetrated by bad hackers. They have the public's best interest at heart.

Good hackers will work within a company's network to find weaknesses in their infrastructure and show the company where potential threats may come up. Ethical hackers have the same tools and knowledge as malicious hackers, but choose to use their skills in a manner that will help instead of destroy an organization. Ethical hacking is most closely associated with **"penetration testing"**.

Penetration Testing

What is penetration testing? It is a type of security testing that is conducted to find out how secure a certain network or computer application is. The purpose of penetration testing is to find out where weaknesses may exist in company's infrastructure.

If the company's network and systems are not secured, a hacker may be able to access private information that is on that system and harm the infrastructure of the company. Penetration testing needs to be performed on a regular basis to ensure that a company's infrastructure is functioning properly on all levels. Testing should be performed whenever:

- Implementing a new policy
- Adding new systems and processes
- Changing network infrastructure
- Moving to a different office location
- Installing new software systems

In order to properly execute testing you must follow a carefully outlined plan to ensure that every area is accounted for. See the following 6 step testing process:

1.) Prep and Planning Stage
2.) Reconnaissance Stage
3.) Discovery Stage
4.) Analyze Discovery and Outline Potential Risks
5.) Penetration Attempts Stage
6.) Final Conclusion Analysis & Report

Prep and Planning Stage

This is the initial stage for penetration testing. It begins by outlining the goals of the testing and the process. The company and the tester will go through a list of the objectives and step by step procedures to complete the testing. After everything is completed they will outline the final solution to improve the system architecture. It may look like this with the process being detailed and identifying specific parts to test.

Goal: *Identifies the goal of the testing investigation*

Process: *Outlines the specific step by step process to get the testing complete*

Solution: *After the testing, the proposed solution to fix the issue is presented*

Reconnaissance Stage

This is the information gathering stage. This includes analyzing the current available information given by the company. This can include the current infrastructure setup, network plans, and current utilized software. This is done to get an idea of how the current setup is structured.

Discovery Stage

This is the stage in which a tester will use tools to scan the network and test for vulnerabilities. They will typically use a mix of manual and automated tools to scan parts of the network to look for flaws. There are typically 4 types of testing that are done in the discovery stage:

- Internal Testing
- External Testing
- Targeted/Specific Testing
- Blind Testing

Internal Testing

This type of attack is something that can be done within the organization. This can be a pissed off employee who has standard authorized user access to a company's systems. This test is done to see how much potential damage an employee can do.

External Testing

This type of penetration testing can target the company's servers and external devices such as their firewalls, web servers, email servers and domain name servers. This is done to see if an attacker can penetrate the system and how far they can go.

Targeted/ Specific Testing

This type of penetration testing is done to an isolated part of an organization to see its vulnerabilities compared to the rest of the infrastructure. Sometimes penetration testing may be short because testing is only being conducted for a specific function or part of the infrastructure.

Blind Testing

Blind testing is very unique. It's a type of testing that is done at a random time to a random part of an organization. Typically no one is aware that this testing will be conducted. It is not scheduled like the other type of testing and it is meant to simulate a real attack that may be done by a real hacker. There is another variations of this attack in which only a few people within the organization are aware that the attack will actually be happening.

Analyze Discovery and Outline Potential Risks

This is the testing assessment stage. The testers will analyze the information that was gathered before and during the penetration testing. This is typically the most time consuming stage in the testing process. Some of the things that will be analyzed and assessed are:

- The risk to the system
- Time required to fix the potential issues
- Associated costs required to fix current issues

Penetration Attempts Stage

This is perhaps the most important stage of all. In this stage, the steps taken to penetrate the system successfully are outlined. This will outline the extent to which the system is vulnerable. This goes hand in hand with the discovery stage and determines where the most vulnerable part of the system is. In order to conduct proper clean up procedures, this stage needs to be carefully outlined.

Final Conclusion Analysis & Report

This stage outlines everything from start to finish and maps out all the steps that have been completed throughout the testing process. The risks are outlined in a detailed report and presented to the company with proposed solutions and cost breakdown. The following points are addressed in the report.

- Comprehensive summary of the completed penetration testing
- Step by step procedure taken during the penetration testing
- The different type of testing that was conducted

- Details of the vulnerabilities of the system and the potential risk involved
- Proposal for fixing the current setup and optimizing the infrastructure
- Proposal for scheduled penetration testing maintenance

By conducting a structured and organized penetration test, a company can ensure that their systems are kept tightly secured and up to par with current technological demands.

BAD HACKING

Whenever there is good in the world, there will also be bad. Bad hacking is something done to a network, individual website, server or person with malicious intent. Bad hackers, or commonly known as black hats, can send attacks in order to do something that will cause intentional harm. Here are some examples:

- Steal your identity
- Corrupt data
- Spread computer viruses and malware
- Steal important information
- Steal money

The list of bad things that hackers can do can get pretty long. The internet is one of the best ways to communicate, share information, transact business and grow your knowledge. Unfortunately, the internet is an easy access point for criminals. As the internet continues to expand and grow, it will create more opportunities for cyber-crime to grow as well.

Cyber-crime has been increasing at an insane rate. Recent reports by Experian have stated that online identity theft increased 300% from 2014-2016. It can be committed against individuals, government entities, business organizations, and property. Let's take a look at some of the most common hacking techniques.

- DDOS Attack
- Key-logging
- DOS Attack
- Phishing
- Waterhole Attacks
- Fake WAP
- Virus, Trojan Attacks
- Click-jacking attacks
- Cookie Theft
- Bait and switch

All of these attacks have the power to seriously harm individuals, businesses, networks, and property. We will be going into further detail of all these attacks in another chapter. These types of attacks can have serious legal implications and should be treated with the highest regard.

HACKING VS.CRACKING

Hacking and cracking. These are two completely different things. They are similar in the fact that they are both malicious forms of cyber activity. We are already familiar with what hacking is, but what is cracking and how do the two differ?

Cracking is when someone breaks into a computer system, typically on a network. This can be done for money, because it's a challenge, or with malicious intent. It's an act of breaking and entering into a system with the goal of pointing out a weakness in the system. Cracking doesn't involve as much skill as hacking does.

What is the difference between the two? A hacker can change the build and functionality of a network or program, while a cracker simply tries to break into a system with hundreds of attempts. An example of cracking would be tricking a system into thinking that a certain process has occurred when in actuality it hasn't. Another example would be cracking into an account that you don't have the password to.

Cracking involves playing tricks on systems in order to find some sort of backdoor entry into the software or network. Cracking can be used in penetration testing to find weaknesses in how a system is built and structured.

Cracking is generally considered less malicious than hacking. Both can be used to improve network stability and how infrastructure interacts with end users, and they can also be used to corrupt data and cause mayhem.

THE UNDEFINED SIDE OF HACKING

You have to first ask yourself the question, why am I hacking ? Am I doing this purely for entertainment to test and further my skills, or am I doing this to get something that I want and cause harm to others in the process?

Many people don't know why they begin hacking in the first place. They may have seen movies that glorify hackers and the skill required to be called a hacker, but they are really not aware of the work ethic involved to become a truly skilled hacker.

It can take years for people to develop the necessary skills and discipline to become a well rounded hacker. For those few that become dedicated to the craft, hacking can present huge opportunities and also huge risks. It all starts with the intent.

Many people believe that there is a very thin line between ethical hacking and malicious hacking and this can be true, if the intent is unclear. Intent is the dividing line between ethical hackers and malicious hackers. It's what separates ethical hackers from cybercriminals.

ETHICAL & LEGAL IMPLICATIONS OF HACKING

The word **"hacking"** tends to carry a negative connotation amongst many people. Ethics in any industry will develop and change over time. Ethical hacking may appear as an oxymoron to most, but it can be very valuable to big organizations.

Many companies around the world employ ethical hackers to protect their systems and data from being stolen by malicious individuals. The internet is the biggest place for confidential and personal information, which opens up a lot of room malicious individuals and organizations to commit cyber-crime.

The legal ramifications for malicious hacking are very serious and should not be taken lightly. Cyber-crime is committed on a daily basis and is becoming increasingly difficult to detect. Many people may be a victim to it and have no idea it is happening to them. Here are some examples where cyber-crime may occur.

- Internet Chat Rooms
- Emails
- Mobile Phones
- Online Notice Boards
- Social networks

A recent report by the McAfee security company estimates that the annual damage to the global economy due to cyber-crime is upwards of 500 billion. Cyber-crime will only continue to increase as the overall internet expands. Let's take a look at some of the common cyber-crimes that happen on a daily basis.

- Financial theft
- Espionage

- Extortion
- Identity Theft
- Credit Card Theft
- Online Drug Trafficking

Cyber-crime is a criminal offense which can have steep penalties. Computer related crimes can range from short 90 day jail sentences for small Class A misdemeanors, to 15-20 years in jail for Class C felonies.

The current legislation for cyber-criminals can be easily exploited by most skilled hackers. In countries such as the Philippines, the current laws against cybercrime are full of holes and present huge opportunities for hackers to set up shop. For the most part, hackers can remain undetected in countries that have weak cyber-crime laws. Even if they do get caught they can typically avoid extradition or imprisonment.

CLASSIFICATIONS OF CYBER- CRIME

Cyber-crime can be best split into four main categories:

- Computer Fraud
- Cyber-ware
- Cyber-Extortion
- Cyber-terrorism

Computer Fraud

Computer fraud is typically some sort of online scam in which hackers either gain access to users systems do defraud them, or trick them into giving them access to personal information. This is where majority of identity theft occurs. The internet is often used as a gateway for hackers to present people with fraudulent solicitations, fraudulent transactions and much more. This can happen on any website. Let's take a look at some of the common computer fraud that happens on a daily basis:

- Email Fraud
- Money-transfer fraud (wires)

- Charity Fraud
- SEO services fraud (Search-Engine-Optimization services)
- Phishing
- Website redirects
- Credit Card Fraud

These are just a few of the computer frauds out there. The list can go on and on. It is important to be aware of where fraud has the possibility to happen so you can know what to avoid online in order to protect yourself.

Cyber Warfare

Cyber-warfare is action taken by another country or state with the purpose of penetrating their networks in order to gain valuable information or cause serious damage. This is done in order to protect a countries cyber-security network with the end goal of reducing the number of cyber-attacks from other countries. Below are the levels in which cyber-warfare can occur.

- Civil
- Private-Sector
- Public-Sector
- Non-Profit
- Military
- Hacktivist groups such as **Anonymous**

Cyber Extortion

Cyber extortion occurs when a certain hacking group or individual hackers send specific threats in order to get something they want. The threats can include the following:

- Exploiting security weaknesses that can cause serious harm to a company's network

- Blackmail to release harmful information about someone in exchange for money

Cyber Terrorism

Cyber terrorism is when hackers attack and intimidate governments or organizations to change their political agenda and objectives. These types of activities can also be aimed an individuals. This will typically be some sort of computer based attack with a specific threat. They can include bomb threats, blackmail, robberies, stock-manipulation threats and much more.

THE LANGUAGES

In order for hackers to work their magic, they need to be fluent in at least one programming language. Expert hackers will be fluent in almost every programming language available out there. The more languages that you know how to code in, the more things you will have the potential to hack.

Today there are literally hundreds of thousands of pre-built programs already available to make hacking automatic, but they are not always 100% safe and effective. If you plan to only use pre-built programs, you will remain an amateur and have the potential to get caught.

If you plan on becoming a pro you must take the time to become fluent in multiple languages. Knowing how to code in different languages will help you cover your tracks in certain scenarios and remain anonymous.

So which is the best recommended programming language for hacking? Becoming a skilled hacker means being well rounded in multiple programming languages so you have ability to adjust to any situation that may come up. Let's take a look at some of the common programming languages related to hacking:

Web Hacking

- PHP
- HTML
- JavaScript
- SQL

Exploit Writing

- Ruby on Rails
- Python

- C++

There are hundreds of different programming languages. If you are just starting out on your journey to hacking, the easiest and most effective language to start off with is Python. See the link below for a long list of programming languages.

https://dzone.com/articles/big-list-256-programming

PHP

PHP used to stand for **"Personal Home Page"**, but now stands for **"Hypertext Pre-Processor"**. PHP is a programming language that is primarily used on server-side scripting. It is used to collect data, generate content, send and receive cookies. It is mainly used in web development with the goal of allowing developers to create web pages quickly and effectively. PHP scripts are used in the following:

- Writing Desktop Applications
- Command line Scripting
- Server-side Scripting

HTML

HTML stands for **"Hyper-Text Markup Language"**. HTML is primarily used to create dynamic web pages and web applications. HTML describes how a specific web page is structured. It is used by standard web browsers to interpret text, images, visuals and audio on a web page.

JavaScript

JavaScript is one of the most popular programming languages around. It is used to make web pages more dynamic and interactive with users. JavaScript is meant to add behavior to a web page and make it interact with the users. It is commonly used in conjunction with HTML to make web applications and pages come to life. JavaScript is supported by major web browsers such as Chrome, Fire-Fox, and Internet Explorer.

SQL

What is SQL? SQL stands for **"Structured Query Language"**. SQL is designed to manage data that is stored in a database. SQL uses data definition and manipulation language to query data for analytics. SQL is very dynamic in helping to pull structured data by storing procedures and having the ability to edit those procedures. It is used by many firms to query data that they need for reporting and analytics. The primary functionality of SQL is driven by **"queries"**, which are a set of operations used to retrieve specific data from the tables that are stored in SQL.

Ruby on Rails

Ruby on rails is a dynamic server-side web application development framework which provides the base structures for majority of databases, web-based services and web pages. It gives developers structure for the code they write. It helps in the development of website applications because it simplifies most tasks.

Python

Python is one of the most widely used programming languages around. It is a great starting point for newbies because its syntax allows hackers to express concepts in less lines of code than other languages. It makes writing lines of code more clear than other languages. Python can be embedded into many other existing applications which give it extreme flexibility. It has powerful functionality due to the fact that it has pre-built libraries for coding.

C++

Like Python, C++ is also one of the most popular and widely used programming languages today. C++ is an object oriented programming language. C++ is most useful in creating everyday applications such as desktop applications, server side applications, SQL server applications and performance based applications. Let's take a look at what C++ is used in:

- Financial Software
- Video Games
- Traffic Lights
- Server Monitoring Applications
- Graphical user interfaces
- Calculators

As a hacker, becoming skilled in any one of these programming languages can make you a threat. Becoming even moderately skilled in all of them can make you a serious threat. Knowing each one will help you adjust in when different situations come up. Get to learning!!!

THE HACKING MENTALITY

Can anyone develop a hacking mentality? Hacking is not for the faint of heart. If you want to become a skilled hacker you have to begin to develop a curiosity about how everything works. You have to almost have an obsessive personality to truly become a master of your craft. You have to fail many times and be happy to do so in order to learn all the intricacies of hacking.

Begin by slowly identifying problems that may exist in the way something is structured or coded. Become focused and obsessed with finding problems on a daily basis and pointing them out. Once you find a potential problem, start compiling a list of possible solutions. If there are people in your circle that can propose quick solutions, interact with them and learn quickly. You definitely don't want to spend hours digging for a solution when someone can help you out with one in five minutes.

Hacking involves the ability to take highly calculated risks. Once you have a list of possible solutions, weigh them against each other to see which one poses that smallest risk. Once you have the final plan, you need some serious balls to execute. Hacking is very risky in general, but being aware of all the possible outcomes ahead of time will help you protect yourself.

Once you have solved the problem look for alternatives that may be more efficient. It is also very important to share your knowledge with others so ideas can be exchanged and other possible solutions can be presented.

BEING PATIENT

Not only do you have to be highly determined, diligent, and laser focused, you have to develop the necessary patience to see your ideas and skills come to fruition. You don't have to know all the answers right away, but you have to understand that this is a journey and being patient with progress is ideal.

SYSTEMATIC

When you are first starting out it is important to have a working model of all the moving parts of a network or system. Hackers need to be highly analytical and grasp new concepts very quickly in order to prevail. If you want to become a highly skilled hacker or programmer you will have to learn to become highly reactive to problems when they pop up.

There are always multiple ways around a problem. Being aware of multiple solutions to a problem is highly valuable in case your first assumption fails. Having a highly systematic way of solving programming issues can help you become highly flexible when issues do present themselves. Map out your solutions and variables and you will become self-efficient and reliable.

DIFFERENT TYPES OF SCANNERS

Port Scanning

A port scanner is a program or application specifically designed to go in and probe a server or host for possible open ports. What is a port? A port is an endpoint of communication in an operating system. It is a 16-digit-bit integer that is associated with an IP address. Each IP address has a corresponding port number: It may look like this:

110.541.999:**1050**

The IP = 110.541.999
The Port= 1050

As you can see here the port is the endpoint of the IP address. A port scanner tries to find an active port. Sometimes it is not a direct attack and it is only meant to find available services on a machine. A port sweep tries to do the same exact thing but it will scan across multiple hosts.

If a port is open, you can see which services are running on the system. In order to use a port scanner you will need to have working knowledge of **TCP/IP**. Let's take a look at some of the common ways a port scanner can be implemented:

- SYN Scan
- TCP Scan
- Windows Scan
- UDP Scan
- ACK Scan

SYN Scan

This is the default scanning option for most users. This is another version of a TCP Scan. A SYN scan creates the actual IP packets and monitors them for a response. These types of scans are often coined as **"half open"** scans because a full TCP connection is never opened.

The scanner creates a SYN packet and if the port is actually open it will respond back with a **"SYN-ACK"** packet. If the port is closed the scanner will respond back with a **"RST"** packet.

This is the most popular and functional type of scan because it allows users to see a clear distinction between open, closed and filtered states.

It also drops the connection before an actual session is created which decreases the chances of being caught.

TCP Scan

TCP stands for **"Transmission Control Protocol"**. This type of scan is typically used when the SYN scan is not an available option. It starts off just like a SYN scan does and if a **"SYN-ACK"** packet is returned, the connections stays active. It ends up responding back with its own **"ACK"** packet and leaves it with the targeted system to terminate the session. Once it terminates the session it will send out a **"RST"** packet. This method is riskier because it has a higher chance of being detected by firewall security and intruder monitoring services.

Windows Scan

This scan is fairly outdated and is not commonly used. It can tell a user if a specific port is open, closed or in a specific filtered state. It's not a very reliable scanning method and should be avoided.

UDP Scan

UDP stands for **"User Datagram Protocol"**. UDP scans are slightly different because they are generally slower and more difficult to implement than regular TCP Scans. It is better suited for transaction oriented queries such as DNS and network time protocol.

ACK Scan

An ACK scan is slightly different than the other scans. It does not search for ports that are open or closed, but instead which ports are filtered or unfiltered. This is used when trying to probe for firewalls.

We have covered the major scanners to help you get an idea of how they work. There are other types of scans that are not commonly used that are worth mentioning:

- Protocol Scan
- Idle Scan
- X-mas Scan
- Proxy Scan
- Null Scan
- Fin Scan
- Maimon Scan
- Cookie Echo Scan
- Custom TCP Scan

Network Scanning

What is network scanning? Networks scanning aims to identify active hosts on a network. It is typically done do either attack the hosts or access them for security purposes. Network scanning returns important information about which IP addresses map to active hosts and the services they are running. Below are some of the phases involved in network scanning:

Foot printing phase: Create a custom profile of the targeted organization (DNS, e-mail servers and IP address range)

Scanning phase: You find out which IP address can be accessed through their system.

Enumeration phase: You will attempt to make active connections to the targeted system and then gather more vital information such as:

- *Specific server settings and configurations*
- *Networks and shared paths*
- *Route Tables*
- *Users and groups*
- *Further DNS details*
- *Software and application use*
- *Alternative Hostnames*

Vulnerability Scanning

A vulnerability scanner is a specific type of computer program that is written to access a computer system or network for weaknesses. By using a vulnerability scanner we can find out the following things about a network:

- The possible flaws of the network
- The hackers access to the flaw
- The ability of the hacker to exploit the flaw in the network

Vulnerability scanning focuses on identifying the current weakness of a network. It then classifies the extent of the weakness. Lastly it comes up with possible solutions to mitigate the access risk to a network. Let's take a look at some examples of what vulnerabilities are related to:

- Hardware
- Software
- Hosting Environment
- Daily operations
- Internal Employee access
- Management

ICMP Scanning/Sweep

ICMP stands for **"Internet Control Message Protocol"**. ICMP is also known as a ping sweep. This technique is used to find out which specific range of IP addresses map to a live host. This is done by sending **"ECHO"** request packets to a targeted host and wait for the ECHO to respond back. Let's take a look at some of the tools that are used to do a ping sweep.

- FPing
- Gping
- Nmap

Once a response is received back it will contain some interesting data. Below is some of the data that is returned back from a ping sweep.

- Packet Loss (the number of packets of data that travel through the network that fail to reach their final endpoint)
- The min, max and average round trip times
- Potential errors during the ping

Below is an example of a ping of yahoo.com

```
C:\WINDOWS\system32\cmd.exe                                          _|□|x|

C:\Documents and Settings\pappu>ping yahoo.com -n 20

Pinging yahoo.com [66.94.234.13] with 32 bytes of data:

Reply from 66.94.234.13: bytes=32 time=341ms TTL=49
Reply from 66.94.234.13: bytes=32 time=350ms TTL=49
Reply from 66.94.234.13: bytes=32 time=339ms TTL=49
Reply from 66.94.234.13: bytes=32 time=341ms TTL=49
Reply from 66.94.234.13: bytes=32 time=340ms TTL=49
Reply from 66.94.234.13: bytes=32 time=338ms TTL=49
Reply from 66.94.234.13: bytes=32 time=340ms TTL=49
Reply from 66.94.234.13: bytes=32 time=338ms TTL=49
Reply from 66.94.234.13: bytes=32 time=337ms TTL=49
Reply from 66.94.234.13: bytes=32 time=342ms TTL=49
Reply from 66.94.234.13: bytes=32 time=336ms TTL=49
Reply from 66.94.234.13: bytes=32 time=337ms TTL=49
Reply from 66.94.234.13: bytes=32 time=337ms TTL=49
Reply from 66.94.234.13: bytes=32 time=346ms TTL=49
Reply from 66.94.234.13: bytes=32 time=341ms TTL=49
Reply from 66.94.234.13: bytes=32 time=340ms TTL=49
Reply from 66.94.234.13: bytes=32 time=336ms TTL=49
Reply from 66.94.234.13: bytes=32 time=338ms TTL=49
Reply from 66.94.234.13: bytes=32 time=338ms TTL=49
Reply from 66.94.234.13: bytes=32 time=337ms TTL=49

Ping statistics for 66.94.234.13:
    Packets: Sent = 20, Received = 20, Lost = 0 (0% loss),
Approximate round trip times in milli-seconds:
    Minimum = 336ms, Maximum = 350ms, Average = 339ms

C:\Documents and Settings\pappu>
```

WIDELY USED TOOLS

Before beginning on this wild journey it is good to familiarize yourself with the industry's most popular hacking tools. Let's take a look at them:

- Kali Linux
- Angry IP Scanner
- Cain & Abel

- Wireshark
- Nmap
- John The Ripper
- Metasploit
- Ettercap

KALI LINUX

What is Kali Linux? Kali-Linux is a Debian-based distribution system that is aimed for high level penetration testing. It is geared towards some of the security tasks below:

- Penetration testing
- Security Research
- Packet Analysis
- Web Security Scanning

Kali Linux contains more than 700 penetration testing tools and systems. It is completely 100% free to use. It is meant to be used for serious penetration testing with large private entities and organizations. Its capabilities stretch far and wide due to all the penetration tools available.

It's under constant development and improvement by the Offensive Security, a leading security training firm. It is available for anyone to use. Below is a site that will give you a full overview of Kali Linux along with installation setups.

http://docs.kali.org/category/introduction

Angry IP Scanner

What is an angry IP scanner? It sounds malicious. It scans IP addresses and their corresponding ports within a specified range. It pings IP addresses to see if they are currently active.

If the hosts that are being pinged do not respond, it typically means that they are dead or inactive. Scanning ports is an integral part of maintaining security and making sure a system is running up to functional standards. Below are some of the supporting platforms Angry IP Scanner can run on.

- Mac OS X
- Linux
- Windows

The link below has a free downloadable version of Angry IP Scanner that you can start using. Please use at your discretion.

http://angryip.org/

Cain & Abel

Cain and Abel is a password recovery tool specifically used for Microsoft Windows. It can recover a variety of different passwords using many different methods. Some of the methods include brute force, packet sniffing, and cryptanalysis.

Wire-Shark

Wireshark is used to analyze network packets. It will try to capture network packets and give as much detailed information as possible about them. It's a measuring tool to help you get an idea of what is actually going on inside a network. Wireshark is open source and relatively easy to use. Below are some examples of what Wireshark is used for.

- Troubleshooting network issues
- Save and open packet data for analysis
- Examine current Network security protocols
- Examine current security problems

Nmap

What is Nmap? Nmap stands for **"Network Mapper"**. It's a security scanner that is used to find hosts and services that are on a network. The main idea is to create a map of the network. This is done by sending custom packets to target hosts and then analyzing their responses. Let's take a look at some of Nmap's other features:

- Network Auditing (identifies new servers)
- Host discovery (finds hosts on a network)
- Network Maintenance
- Auditing Network Connections (monitors incoming/ outgoing connections)

John The Ripper

John the Ripper is one of the most popular and widely used password cracking tools. John the Ripper combines several different cracking programs and runs them together. It is often used in enterprise to sniff out weak passwords that could pose a security risk. John the Ripper was originally developed for Unix, but it is now used for many different platforms.

Metasploit

Metasploit is an open source security system that gives detailed information about possible security vulnerabilities and helps in penetration testing. The Metasploit Framework is used to develop and deploy code against a remote machine. Users can build their own set of specific tools that they want and see fit for their penetration testing. Below are some of the specific tasks you can accomplish with Metasploit:

- Network Scanning
- Packet Sniffing
- Listening to Incoming connections

Metasploit has many more capabilities when combined with other services. It can be customized to create an attack in a very unique way.

Ettercap

Ettercap is another open source network security tool. It is popular for man-in-the middle attacks which we will get to in a later chapter of this book. It is commonly used for network analysis and security auditing. It can sniff out live connections, filter out specific content and provide detailed host analysis. It can be run on the following operating systems:

- Linux
- Mac OS X
- Microsoft Windows
- Solaris

It supports both active and passive attacks which we will also get to in another chapter in this book.

Now that we have basic working knowledge of the most commonly used tools, it's time to learn about some of the different types of attacks.

CHAPTER 3: DIFFERENT TYPES OF ATTACKS

DDOS Attack

DDOS stands for **"Distributed Denial of Service"**. This is when a user's machine services are made unavailable to them. They are one of the most popular types of attacks.

When a certain system is off-line, a hacker can attempt to either corrupt the entire website. They can also attack a separate functionality of the website and use it as they see fit. The goal is to either completely take down a system or temporarily harm a specific part of a website.

DDOS attacks can be sent by multiple devices and distributed through what is known as a botnet. What the heck is a botnet? A **"botnet"** is group or network of devices that have been compromised and used to transmit viruses and malware to other computers on the web. A botnet is commonly referred to as a **"zombie army"**. The reason being is because the owners of the devices are not aware that their devices have been compromised. They are controlled by someone else, usually a cybercriminal.

Let's take a look at some different types of DDOS attacks:

- UDP Flood
- SYN Flood
- Slowloris
- Ping of Death
- Ping Flood
- R.U.D.Y
- HTTP Flood
- DNS Amplification
- IP Fragmentation Attack

This is a long list of attacks and we will briefly describe each one.

UDP Flood

A UDP **(User Datagram Protocol)** flood is a type of a denial-of-service attack which floods random ports on a remote host with tons of UDP packets. This can be sent to a single location or it can be randomized. The goal of this type of attack is to over-flood the firewall with requests.

SYN Flood

A SYN flood is also another type of denial-of-service attack. In this attack a hackers sends a large amount of SYN packets to one port or multiple ports on a targeted server with the goal of using enough server resources to make the system unresponsive.

Slow-loris

Slow-loris is a type of software that is highly targeted. It uses a single computer to take down a targeted web server. The interesting thing about this attack is that it only affects the targeted web server while having no effects on other running services and ports. It opens multiple connections to a web server and keeps them open for long periods of time.

Ping of Death

This type of attack involves sending a modified type of ping which is very malicious. This is another type of denial-of-service attack in which a hacker sends IP packets that are larger than the allowed IP protocol. They attempt to essentially crash the targeted service.

Ping Flood

In this type of attack a hacker sends a ton of Echo Request packets with the goal of overwhelming the system to the point of failure. It will send ICMP packets as fast as possible without waiting for any reply back from the system. This ends up consuming a large amount of bandwidth on the system which results in a denial of service.

R.U.D.Y

Short for **R-U-Dead-Yet**, is a longer term a DOS attack. It is used to send attacks at a slow rate with the goal of opening only a few connections to a targeted server and keeping the sessions open for a longer period of time. These are more difficult to detect from a ping flood because the requests can be randomized and sent across very slowly.

HTTP Flood

An HTTP flood is an attack that is used by hackers to target a web server and its running applications. They are one of the most advanced forms of attacks today. They can be very difficult to detect because the hackers use legitimate forms of HTTP **GET** and **POST** requests to take down a web server.

HTTP floods often use botnets and malware to gain access to a web server. They don't use any modified forms of packets or spoofing techniques and they don't require much bandwidth to do damage. They demand a higher understanding of the web server applications. These types of attacks tend to be very specific when carried out.

DNS Amplification

In this type of attack the hacker targets vulnerabilities in the DNS servers to make small queries increase their payloads with the goal of crashing the servers.

A DNS amplification attack is a type of reflection attack in which the hacker sends out DNS queries to evoke a response from the DNS to a spoofed IP address. These are fake queries that are meant to cause the DNS to respond back to a false IP address to open the DNS resolver. This can seriously bog down a server if false queries are sent back and forth causing the DNS resolver to respond quickly in a short period of time.

IP Fragmentation Attack

This is the process of breaking up an IP datagram into many other packets of smaller and smaller sizes. The attack works by exploiting the mechanisms of datagram fragmentation. Each network will tend to have limits for the size of datagrams that it can process.

This is known as the maximum transmission unit **(MTU).** If a certain datagram is being sent and is larger than the MTU, it will need to be fragmented down in order to be sent across accordingly. Attacks like this will tend to manipulate datagrams in a way that will exploit the MTU and slow down processes on the server.

DOS ATTACK

A DOS attack is short for **"Denial-of- Service"** attack. This is a type of network attack that is meant to take down the network or machine and make it unavailable to users. One way this is done is by flooding the network with useless traffic.

DOS attacks can come in many different ways. They can target a direct service that is running or the server altogether. DOS attacks don't really try to get important information. They just attempt to make certain services unavailable to users. Let's take a look at how DOS attacks are sectioned off:

- Network Layer Attacks
- Application Layer Attacks

Network Layer Attacks

Network layer attacks are very traffic intensive. They focus on slowing down connections to your network by spamming the server with request.

Some attacks include the following:

- UDP Flood
- SYN Flood
- DNS Amplification

Once successfully implemented, these attacks can take down access to the server.

Application Layer Attacks

These types of attacks can vary from DOS to DDOS. The main goal behind an application layer attack is to overload the server by spamming it with a heavy amount of request that require a lot of processing power. In order to understand how these application layer attacks work you need to understand how they are measured.

Application layer attacks are measured in RPS. RPS stands for **"Request Per Second".** For small to mid-sized websites, 40 to 100 RPS are enough to take them down and make their service unavailable. Let's take a look at some typical application layer attacks:

- HTTP floods
- R.U.D.Y
- DNS amplification

Reasons behind a DDOS/DOS attack

Why do DDOS and DOS attacks happen? What would motivate someone to hack a network or take down a particular server? There are plenty of reasons. There is always some motivation driving an attack. Attacks can be launched from a single user, businesses, and even government entities. Let's look at some common intentions of hacking:

- Vandalism
- Hacktivism
- Friendly competition

- Business Intent
- Extortion

**Vandalism** – _Most online vandalism happens on the low level of the hacking spectrum. These types of attacks are usually driven by rookies. They will typically use pre-made scripts and code to do simple attacks that don't require a ton of skill. The motivation can be just go get an adrenaline rush or prove your skills to someone. The attacks are never really too drastic because most low level DDOS mitigation service will catch it before it really becomes a problem. It can be as something as silly as changing around letters of a website, messing with the font or writing something rebellious on the website to prove a point._

**Hacktivism-** _Hacktivists like the group **Anonymous** usually don't hack for malicious intent, but rather to expose controversial information or prove a point to wide audience. They are typically more advanced hackers who want to have a voice and make sure people know that they exist._

**Friendly Competition/Rivalry-** _Be careful who you piss off. You never know who is secretly a skilled hacker on the side. Some people hack in order to get back at someone for something they previously did to them. This often happens when someone wants to get revenge on someone. It can happen on social networking sites, gaming sites, dating sites, etc. This can include password cracking to get access to someone's social media account and other things that can sabotage someone's reputation._

**Business Intent** _–Believe it or not, businesses that are in direct competition with each other will hack each other in order to remain number one. A DDOS attack or DOS attack can cost companies a ton of money. Some companies can't afford to have their website go down for more than a few minutes without it affecting their bottom line._

While a company's website is down, it can prevent them from taking part in a specific event or function that can cripple their business and growth potential. Hackers can cause the user experience on a website to be terrible in terms of site load time, order processing, and much more. This can often cause customers to flee to other companies.

Extortion – _This is a very popular motive for hackers. This is where a hacker demands cash in return for stopping their attack or further damage they plan to inflict on the users system. These typically come in the form of a DDOS attack._

IP SPOOFING

IP spoofing is a technique in which a hacker masks himself as a trusted host to a network with the intent to hijack a website, browser or specific function of a site. This kind of process is not easy to do and requires some skill. So how is this process carried out?

The way computer networks communicate with each other is by exchanging data packets. These data packets contain **"headers"** which are used to route the transmission of data. The **"Source IP Address"** is an example of a header. The source IP address indicates the IP address that sent the original packet.

IP spoofing starts off with the hacker obtaining the IP address of the real host and altering the packet headers. By altering the packet headers, the legit host looks like the actual source. It is most commonly deployed in network layer attacks. IP spoofing is commonly used when a hacker is trying to hide the location of a botnet and when attempting to generate fake requests from the target source.

Common forms of IP spoofing include:

- DNS spoofing
- IP spoofing
- ARP spoofing

MAN-IN-THE MIDDLE (MITM) (MIM) (MitM)

In this type of attack a hacker acts as the middleman of a real time transaction or conversation between two other parties. They are impersonating both sides of an organization with the goal of gaining access to valuable information that the original parties were trying to communicate over to each other.

In this situation a hacker is intercepting important information from two parties without them really having any idea its happening. The data is meant for someone else, they just happen to be in the middle of it while it's getting transmitted between two parties. Once a hacker intercepts a live session between two parties, it becomes extremely dangerous because the hacker can manipulate information that is vital to an organization.

A common method used in Man in the Middle attacks is through the distribution of malware. Once a hacker has direct control over the user's web browser they can easily take over transactions and conversations.

LOGIC BOMB

Don't get scared. Nothing is going to explode here with a logic bomb. What is a logic bomb and how does it work? A logic bomb is a piece of code that is written and placed in a system that will execute or **"explode"** under certain criteria.

The criteria can be for the code to execute its function after a certain period of time has elapsed or after a certain action is performed on the system. For example, a logic bomb can be placed on a system to display a cryptic message after 30 minutes of being inserted.

A logic bomb can come in the form of virus, worm or Trojan horse. It can also be coded to corrupt certain data or information following a specific action from the user such as logging into a certain system, accessing a certain type of file, or logging into their bank to capture certain data.

Logic bombs can be very serious and are an advanced form of hacking because they require specifically crafted code in order to execute. Majority of the time logic bombs are purely of malicious intent.

Let's take a look at some of the criteria that can cause a logic bomb to activate:

- Certain amount of time has elapsed since insertion
- A certain amount of disc space has filled up on the system
- Data has been altered or deleted
- A certain site being accessed

There are so many different types of logic bombs out there and the reason being is because the hacker can specify the logic under which they execute. Most security detection software will catch them before they set off, but they are worth noting.

VIRUS

A virus is one of the most popular topics around in the world of programming and computers. You may have seen movies such as Swordfish that glorify viruses and skew the reality behind what they really are and how they work. Our modern culture opens up viruses every day without even knowing it. So what is exactly is a computer virus and how does it work?

A computer virus is a malicious piece of code or program that is designed to spread to multiple computers and cause issues to the system such as destroying data, corrupting files, and even taking down entire networks. Viruses tend to attach themselves to executable files and only infect your computer once that file or program is executed.

Viruses will spread with the push of human action. They can take a longer time to spread but it can depend on the type of virus that is being executed. Most people will continue to spread viruses without really knowing that they are doing it.

WORM

A worm is form of virus that self-replicates itself with the goal of spreading to other computers. It usually does this by using a network to spread across and tends to consume a ton of bandwidth. The goal of a worm is not to modify the system it goes through, but simply to keep on spreading to as many computers as possible.

How do worms spread? They spread by finding some sort of weakness or vulnerability in the operating systems they go through. They also tend to delete files and install backdoors on computers they access. You should be very cautious when you visit network sharing sites because it's a good point of access for worms to replicate.

There are different types of worms that can attach themselves to your computer and allow cybercriminals to have remote access to your computer. Worms are efficient because they do not need human action to continue spreading. So once a worm begins spreading successfully it can do a lot of damage before it gets caught. The rate at which a worm can spread across to other computers can be alarming.

TROJAN HORSE

A Trojan horse can be pretty tricky. At first glance it can appear to be a useful piece of software that you plan on using for something, but once it gets installed on your system it can seriously damage your computer. It is meant to mislead the receiving user of its true intentions. If you are on the receiving end of a Trojan horse you are usually tricked into opening the software because it seems legitimate from a trusted source.

Trojans are spread by getting users to execute a certain routine such as opening an attachment, downloading a program or even filling out a form of some sort. This can allow a hacker to get access to personal information that they were searching for such as passwords, IP addresses, bank information, mailing address etc.

Trojans typically do not try to insert themselves to other files on the system or replicate themselves like a virus or worm. They are typically used for slightly different activity. Let's take a look at some of their purposes and capabilities:

- **Data theft** (passwords, credit card info, personal information, social security numbers, bank information, corporate data info)
- **Spying and surveillance** (monitoring users actions, key-logging, remote control of users system)
- **Malicious intent** (data corruption, malware insertion, data deletion, file modification, crashing a network or system)

These are just a few of the capabilities of a Trojan. There are more advanced uses like setting up botnet and performing automated attacks on a network. This requires an experienced skillset and a serious appetite for causing mayhem.

Now that we have a solid understanding of the different types of attacks out there, let's dive into the fun stuff. We will go over some basic types of hacking procedures that are meant to be for educational uses only and to be used at your full discretion.

CHAPTER 4: STEP BY STEP PROCEDURES

BEWARE!!!

Hacking can get you into some serious trouble if you don't cover your tracks. These tips are provided to you for educational use ONLY!!! Use them at your discretion and assume the risks that come along with them. This is provided to you for ethical use only and I advise against using hacking for malicious intent.

Hacking does carry a human element and therefor errors can be common if you aren't careful. If you don't know what you are doing you can cause serious issues to your system. If you decide to go beyond this point you assume all responsibility and possible legal repercussion.

PASSWORD HACKING AND LOGIN ACCESS

Hackers get a kick out of breaking passwords and getting access to just about anything. They tend to shift their focus to less secured sites that are fairly new and upcoming. They can also target subsites of major sites that have flaws in design and login access.

We have all lost our password to an email login, bank login or social media account at one point or another in our lifetime. This can be very frustrating and a perfect opportunity for a hacker to attack and steal your information. So what do you do if you find yourself locked out of one of your accounts that you need to access? The great thing is that you have options for recovery. Let's take a look at two of the most popular options for recovery.

Option 1 – The Windows Password Recovery Tool

For this option you will need to use a secondary computer and something that you can save the software on that you will be using. You can use USB flash drive or a CD/DVD. This recovery tool has 4 different versions that you can use: Standard, Pro, Enterprise, and the Ultimate. Below is the website that you need to visit to get started

http://www.windowspasswordsrecovery.com/windows-password-recovery-tool.html

All the versions are paid, but you can test the free versions out of each edition. This is compatible for majority of Windows systems. This tool is effective and easy to use in order to hack your own password.

It works quickly without any risk of viruses and damages being done to your computer. The tool works to reset, remove or change domain admin access for passwords of other users. If your previous account was hacked you can easily create a new domain admin access account to fix the issue. It currently supports the following desktops, laptops and table PC'S below:

- HP
- Dell
- Sony
- Lenovo
- ASUS

Let's take a look at the step by step procedure as to how it works.

Step 1) Download and Install

1.) You can download a free trial version of any of the edition on the website below. I would suggest you download the Standard version trial of this. It works the easiest and is less complex than all the others.

http://www.windowspasswordsrecovery.com/getting_started/

2.) Click the downloaded file to install the standard version. Feel free to install this on any PC you want. Once downloaded click **Next** to install.

3.) Once the software is installed make sure to enable the **"Run Windows Tool Standard"**. After that click **"Finish"**. Once this is done the tool will launch itself automatically.

Step 2) Burn Recovery Tool to CD/DVD or USB

The Standard version offers you two alternatives to create a functional CD/DVD drive: The Quick Recovery mode with default IOS image file, or the advanced Recovery Wizard with the new IOS image file. For this please use the Quick Recovery mode with the default IOS image file that is given by the Windows Recovery Tool.

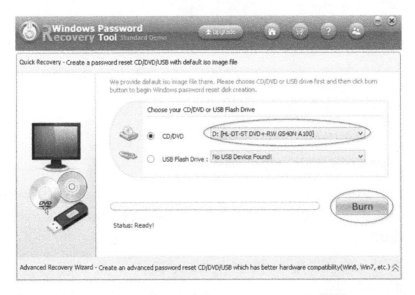

Have a disc in the CD/DVD drive and the select **"BURN"**. After you select burn you might receive a little message that says **"Disc is not blank. Do you want to erase it now"?** If this pops up, please select yes.

This is what it will look like if it pops up.

Once the password reset CD/DVD has been successfully created, you will get the following message below confirming that it has been created. Once this pops up select okay to continue to the next step.

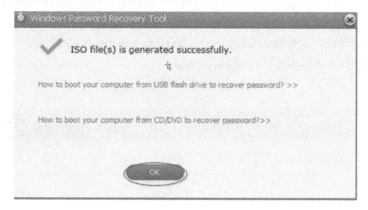

Step 3) Remove your Windows password

Now that you created the CD/DVD, insert it and reboot your computer to begin. Once the CD/DVD reboots, you will see that the program is initializing.

After it loads, the Password Recovery Tool Menu will load up again and you will need to select the system you wish to reset the password for and then click **"NEXT"**.

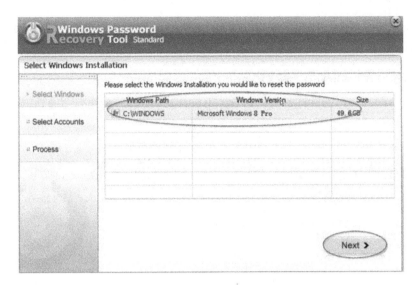

Once you have selected the path and clicked next, the following menu
will pop up below.

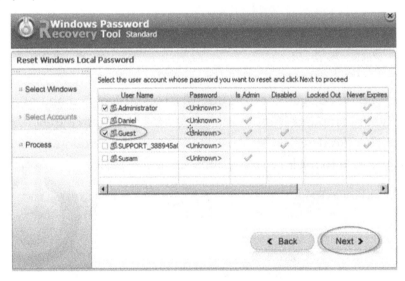

Once it pops up, select the user accounts whose password you wish to
reset and click **"NEXT"** to reset. You will see all the current user names of
your accounts that are currently available with the password status
showing as either **"UNKNOWN"** or **"EMPTY"**. If the status displays as
unknown it means you have a password for that username, but you may
have lost it. If the status displays as empty it means that you don't have a

password for that username and you can login the account without a password.

Once you have clicked **"NEXT"** and the password has been removed successfully you will receive a congratulations message like the one below.

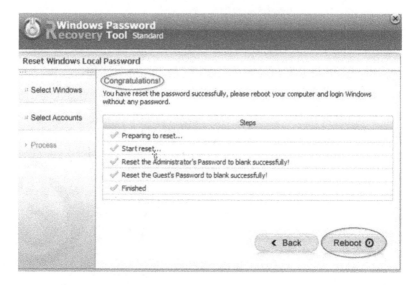

Once this menu pops up click **"REBOOT"** to restart your computer and login to your computer without using a password. Remove the CD/DVD and click the **"RESTART NOW"** button to restart the computer. After this you will be able to log into your computer without using a password.

Option 2 – Command Prompt

So what if you are already logged in but need to figure out the password for another one of your accounts. Not to worry, there is a solution for this. This is a much simpler way to do this through the command prompt of your computer. Let's take a look.

Step 1) Open up your computers Command Prompt

You can open your computers command prompt by going to your start menu and typing in either **"command"** or **"cmd"** in the search box. Once the option for the command prompt comes up, right click and run as **administrator**. Below is what it will look like.

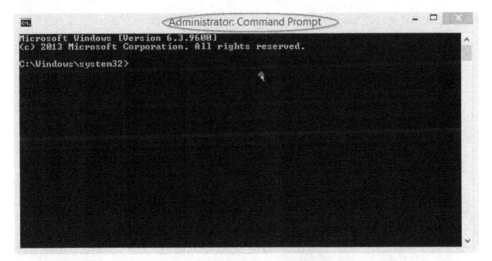

Step 2) Type in **"net user"** in the command prompt and click enter.

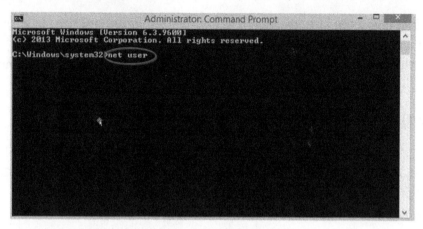

After you hit enter you will see the following pop up.

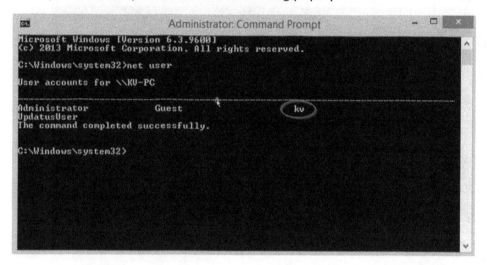

You can see that there are two users on this system, **guest** and **kv**. If I wanted to change the password for the username **kv** I would type in the following command in the command prompt shown on the next page.

Net user kv "NewPassword" <<< this would be what you select your new password to be. See how it looks below if I chose my new password for that username to be **"ilovetacos"**.

Net user kv ilovetacos

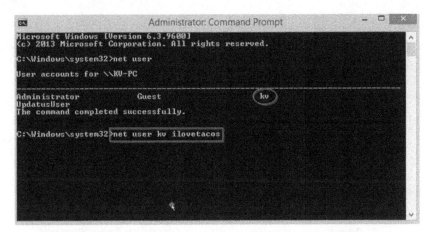

Once you type this in and then press enter, the password for that username will get changed. You will get the following confirmation below once the password gets changed.

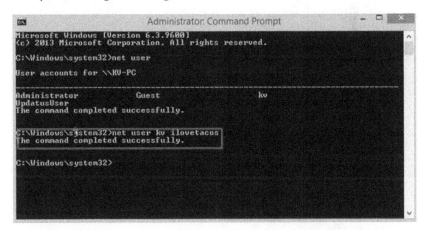

This can be very helpful if you have forgotten the password on a specific account. Cracking the password to a specific website or someone else's systems is completely different and way more labor intensive. There is software out there that can do this for you, but it costs thousands upon thousands of dollars.

I have to share something interesting that happened to me as I was writing this book and putting the password reset tutorial together. As I was doing the demo for resetting your password in the command prompt, I accidently reset my password and totally forgot what I reset it to. It was not the password I show in the demo. I relentlessly tried to remember it, but was having no luck. I had locked myself out of my own computer. The irony was comical.

I figured I should have no issue resetting it as I have just created a guide for it in the book. So what I ended up doing was going to the Microsoft website and getting the free version of the Windows Password Recovery Tool. I used my laptop for this since I was locked out of my computer.

I burned the program on a disc and proceeded to use it to reset my password. I did not think I would encounter as many issues as I did. I am running Windows 8 and Windows 8 doesn't happen to be compatible with most password recovery tools out there. Unfortunately when I tried to use the Windows Password Recovery Tool it did not work. I tried 5 different kinds of programs that I downloaded online and none of them ended up working. Below are the 5 that I tried and did not work for me.

- Kon-Boot
- Cain & Abel
- LCP
- Ophcrack
- Offline NT Password & Registry Editor

The program that ended up working for me after I tried all the other 5 was the Trinity Rescue kit. This ended up being compatible with Windows 8. The other 5 above are more geared towards Windows 7 and versions before that. It was pretty embarrassing, but I was eventually able to get in.

I actually didn't end up resetting my password, but wiping it off completely. That's how the Trinity Rescue kit works. It works in the same fashion as the Windows Password Recovery Tool, but it wipes your password so you can just get in without a password. It edits your registry on your computer so it doesn't require a password upon login. I highly recommend trying the other password recovery tools above if the issue ever happens to you. To avoid having this happen to you, I suggest creating multiple users on your computer and have one that doesn't require a password to get in. Trust me, it could happen when you least expect it. Below you will find the links for all the other tools. My top 2 highest recommendations would be the Trinity Rescue Kit and Offline NT Password & Registry Editor.

Trinity Rescue Kit
http://trinityhome.org/Home/index.php?content=TRINITY_RESCUE_KIT_DOWNLOAD

Kon – Boot

http://www.piotrbania.com/all/kon-boot/index2.html

Cain & Abel

http://www.oxid.it/cain.html

LCP

https://web.archive.org/web/20131021061428/http://www.lcpsoft.com/english/download.html

Offline NT Password & Registry Editor

https://www.lifewire.com/offline-nt-password-and-registry-editor-review-2626147

ANONYMOUS SURFING (TOR)

You really never know who is out there and potentially monitoring your online activity. You could be surfing Youtube or Facebook and someone could be watching you. Nobody wants their privacy invaded or comprised. Thankfully there is a free and viable solution out there. You can remain anonymous online through the use of a Tor browser.

What the heck is Tor?

Tor is a free software which enables you to surf online and remain completely anonymous. Tor uses incoming internet traffic and directs it through a free volunteer network which is layered through thousands of different relays in order to conceal the original location of the user. Tor makes it virtually impossible to track your online identity.

Tor was created to protect the identity and privacy of online users. Tor is commonly referred to as an onion router. This is because it uses encryption in the application layer of the communication stack which mimics layers of an onion. It encrypts incoming data and sends it through a layer of circuits which go through randomized Tor relays. Because of this type of randomized routing that is done when data is relayed back and forth, it makes it nearly impossible to trace back to the original user. This process conceals your online identity.

Tor is also the access point to the dark web. The dark web is an encrypted user network that exists through Tor. The dark web requires special software like Tor in order to access it. Websites on the dark web end with a .onion extension and not .com, .net, .org, like you are commonly used to seeing with a standard web browser.

The dark web can be a very dangerous place if you don't know what you are doing. In order to access it you need to first download a Tor browser. Below is a link to a safe and reliable place where you can download a Tor browser.

https://www.torproject.org/projects/torbrowser.html.en

Once you have downloaded and installed it, you will have a little icon on your desktop that looks like this.

There are many different tutorials online on how to use the Tor browser. Once you learn how to use it, you can change your identity online with just a click of a button. It is extremely easy. The dark web has many dangerous websites that you can access and you should be extremely careful when visiting them.

I REPEAT. EXTREMELY CAREFUL !!!

There are many different websites on there that offer illegal and dangerous products. Below are just a few things that you will see offe red for sale one some sites. Some can be scams and some are 100% legitimate. Visit them at your discretion and be careful what kind of information you give out.

- Drugs
- Guns
- Hackers for Hire
- Passports and Identification
- Stolen Credits Cards

The list can go on and on. I am giving you some sites you can access on Tor, and please note they can get you in some serious trouble. Visit them at your discretion and I advise to only visit them for educational purposes only.

https://darkwebnews.com/deep-web-links/

This site give you access to wide range of websites you can visit on the dark web. Notice how they all end with a .onion extension. You will not be able to access these websites on a standard browser like FireFox or Google Chrome. If you don't' believe me, go ahead and try it for yourself.

Below are some of the different types of websites you may find.

- Financial Services
- Hosting
- Security
- Whistle Blowing
- Hacking
- Hackers for Hire
- Anarchy Sites
- Marketplace Drugs
- Guns
- Crypto Currency

It will blow your mind what kind of websites exist out there that you have yet to visit. For a final time, be EXTREMELY careful when visiting these types of sites. I suggest that you change your identity every time you visit one of these sites.

You can learn how to do this once you have fully installed Tor. Below is a video that will help you navigate Tor and how to use a new IP address anytime you feel like it.

https://www.youtube.com/watch?v=307FUu0XgjU

RESOURCES

We have only scratched the surface into the wild world of hacking. I hope you have enjoyed this journey so far and have learned some valuable lessons. Hacking is an art form. It must be respected and treated with caution and dignity. In order to advance your journey into possibly becoming a skilled hacker, you must continue to do relentless research. I highly advise using the following website below to continue learning and evolving.

https://hackerone.com/blog/resources-for-new-hackers

It is a great resource point to learning new hacking techniques, installing new software and so much more.

I hope you have enjoyed reading this book and have gotten some great information out of it.

www.ingramcontent.com/pod-product-compliance
Lightning Source LLC
LaVergne TN
LVHW092354060326
832902LV00008B/1037